Learn to Play Guitar wi
Metallica

Photo by Ross Halfin

Left to Right: Kirk Hammett, James Hetfield, Lars Ulrich, Jason Newsted

Also available:
Learn to Play Bass with Metallica (02500189)
Learn to Play Drums with Metallica (02500190)

To access audio visit:
www.halleonard.com/mylibrary

Enter Code
3095-9631-7417-8214

Front cover photo by Mark Leialoha
All quotes courtesy of *Guitar One* magazine

ISBN 978-1-57560-280-6

HAL•LEONARD®
CORPORATION
7777 W. BLUEMOUND RD. P.O. BOX 13819 MILWAUKEE, WI 53213

Visit Hal Leonard Online at
www.halleonard.com

Introduction

Learn to Play Guitar with Metallica is perhaps the most practical guitar method you'll come across. Unlike other methods that teach you songs you haven't heard since nursery school, this book will have you playing cool music by Metallica right away, while teaching fundamental music topics such as rhythm, reading, and chords. You'll have so much fun that you won't even realize you're learning "important" stuff. And best of all, you'll sound way better than your friends who have been playing just as long, but who have nothing to show for it besides a lovely rendition of "Mary Had a Little Lamb." This book will also leave you with the skills necessary to play guitar in a band and kick some serious musical booty.

—Joe Charupakorn

Contents

CHAPTER 1

- **Parts of the Guitar**
- **How to Hold the Guitar**
- **How to Tune the Guitar**
- **How to Read Chord Diagrams**
- **How to Read Tablature**
- **How to Read Music**

My first impression of playing the guitar came from my cousin. We were playing down in the basement at my house. We were goofing off like little kids, and all of a sudden he jumped up on this old wooden table and started pretending like he was playing guitar. He was making guitar sounds. I looked up at him, and I thought, "Wow, he's really cool, doing that." —Kirk Hammett

Introduction

This book is designed to be used without a teacher, so you can work at your own pace. Read through the text for each section, listen to the corresponding musical examples, and then try to play the examples yourself either alone or with the audio. If something is difficult for you to play, don't give up on it—just slow it down until you can master it and then gradually speed up your playing of the selection until it matches that of the track. Don't skip over to the next section until you have mastered the previous one. Try to work and practice for half an hour each day, but even if you can only clear a few minutes every day to play, you'll progress steadily in your technique and be kicking serious musical booty in no time.

Parts of the Guitar

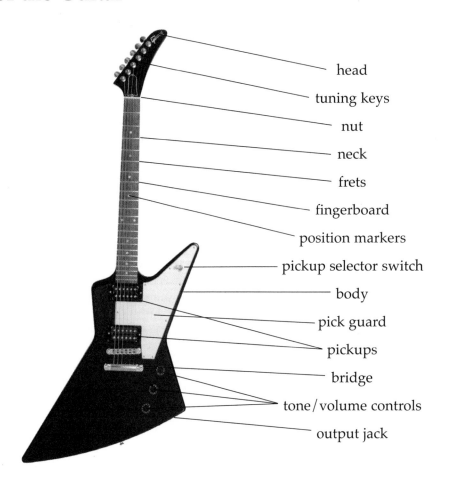

- head
- tuning keys
- nut
- neck
- frets
- fingerboard
- position markers
- pickup selector switch
- body
- pick guard
- pickups
- bridge
- tone/volume controls
- output jack

How to Hold the Guitar

This book assumes that you are playing right-handed. If you are left-handed, mentally substitute "left" for "right" and vice versa as you read this book. If you are sitting, rest the body of the guitar on your right leg. If you are standing, make sure the guitar is strapped securely and is at a comfortable height. Although being strapped low is *de rigueur* for rockers, it puts the left hand in an awkward position that makes playing difficult.

Sitting

Standing

The left hand is used to *fret* notes. You fret a note when you place a finger on a string between two frets (thin metal bars running acros the neck) of the guitar. The thumb should be centered behind the neck with the fretting fingers, curved and with the knuckles bent, on the fretboard. Do not let the left hand palm touch the back of the guitar neck.

Left Hand Correct Positioning (Front)

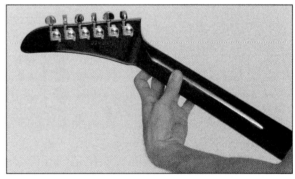

Left Hand Correct Positioning (Back)

Using the thumb and index finger of your right hand, hold the pick with a loose, fist-like grip.

Right Hand

You play one or more strings at a time by stroking them with the pick. When you play by strumming or plucking downwards with the pick, it is called a *downstroke*. When you strum or pluck upwards, it is called an *upstroke*.

How to Tune the Guitar

Before you play anything on the guitar, the first thing you have to do—and this is very important—is make sure the guitar is in tune. Tuning your guitar by ear is simple.

Conventional tuning of the guitar is as follows. Note that the 6th string is towards the ceiling as you hold the guitar and is the lowest-sounding string of the guitar.

TRACK 1

| E | A | D | G | B | E |
| 6th string | 5th string | 4th string | 3th string | 2nd string | 1st string |

Track 1 includes source pitches for all six notes, beginning on the 6th string and working up to the 1st. Tune each string by adjusting it until its pitch matches the corresponding one on the track.

A common way of tuning the guitar is by using a fixed reference source such as a piano, pitch pipe, or tuning fork. To use a tuning fork, strike it against a hard surface and tune the 5th string to its pitch (most tuning forks sound only one pitch—an A). Then, you can proceed to tune the rest of the strings using the 5th string as a reference, as explained below.

You can tune a guitar to itself when you have a pitch source for only one string (as in the case of a tuning fork) or no pitch source at all. When you do this, the strings are in tune in relation to each other.

To tune a guitar to itself, use the 6th string as the initial pitch. If you're using a tuning fork, in step 1 make sure to tune the 6th string to the 5th, not the 5th to the 6th.

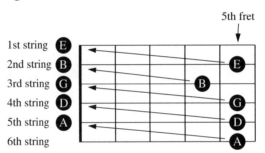

1. Play the 5th fret of the 6th string and then the *open* (i.e., not fretted) 5th string. Adjust the 5th string accordingly until its pitch matches that of the 6th string.

2. Play the 5th fret of the 5th string and then the open 4th string. Adjust the 4th string accordingly until its pitch matches that of the 5th string.

3. Play the 5th fret of the 4th string and then the open 3rd string. Adjust the 3rd string accordingly until its pitch matches that of the 4th string.

4. Play the *4th* fret of the 3rd string and then the open 2nd string. Adjust the 2nd string accordingly until its pitch matches that of the 3rd string.

5. Play the 5th fret of the 2nd string and then the open 1st string. Adjust the 1st string accordingly until its pitch matches that of the 2nd string.

You may notice that there is a sort of pulsing or vibrating sound that occurs when playing two strings simultaneously. When you're tuning one string to match another, your goal is to make this pulse disappear. The closer the two strings get to each other, the longer (and further apart) the pulses will sound. Eventually, the pulses will cease altogether, signaling that they are "in tune" with each other.

One really quick way to get in tune is to use an electronic tuner, which can be bought inexpensively at most music stores. With an electronic tuner, you plug the guitar into the machine, set it to the note of the string you wish to tune, play the string, and adjust the string until the machine indicates that it is in tune (follow the directions of your particular tuner). You should definitely know the old fashioned ways as well, but a tuner will come in handy when you're trying to tune in a loud environment (such as at a rehearsal or gig). A tuner will let you dive right into Metallica's music while you're still learning how to tune by ear.

How to Read Chord Diagrams

A chord diagram is a graphic representation of a small portion of the guitar neck and is used to show the note location and fingering of a specific chord. The perspective of a chord diagram is that of looking at a guitar on a stand in front of you. The horizontal lines represent frets and the vertical lines represent strings. To the right of the diagram is a fret marker that indicates the specific fret where the chord is to be played. The only time you will not see fret markers is in the open position, where the nut is the topmost horizontal line, and the first fret is the line below it. An "o" above the diagram indicates an open string, while an "x" indicates that the string is not to be played at all. A *barre* occurs when you hold down more than one string on the same fret with only one left-hand finger. The numbers below the diagram show which left-hand fingers to use. They are numbered i (index) through 4 (pinky); the thumb is not numbered.

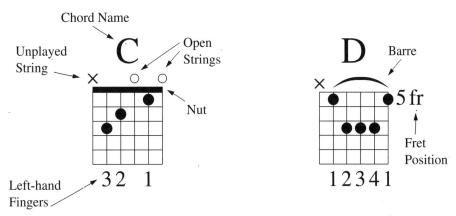

How to Read Tablature

I bought a lot of music books (when I was starting out). Back then it was difficult to learn how to play guitar—much more difficult than it is now. Now, everything that comes out is available in TAB two weeks later.—Kirk Hammett

Tablature graphically displays the string and fret location of any note, allowing guitarists who are not fluent in standard notation, or who do not yet have a strong command of the fretboard, to find quickly specific note locations on the guitar.

The tablature staff has six horizontal lines, corresponding to the guitar's six strings. The bottom line represents the low E string, and each subsequent line going up represents each higher string. The numbers on the lines tell you which fret to press on the particular string. A "0" indicates an open string.

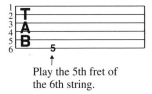

Play the 5th fret of
the 6th string.

The numbers are spaced according to where they fall in the measure (e.g., first note, second note, etc.). If more than one string has a number on it at any given time, then you should play all of the indicated notes simultaneously.

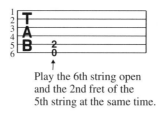

Play the 6th string open
and the 2nd fret of the
5th string at the same time.

Although tablature is not intended to be a replacement for reading conventional music notation (explained below), it does provide one thing standard notation does not always include—an exact fret and string location for each note in a sequence. Since most notes on the guitar can be played on more than one fret and string, tablature is used to offer the best practical fretting for a musical situation.

Warning: Music Theory Ahead!

What follows is a basic overview of the language of music. You don't need to speak the language in order to play the guitar. However, it's difficult to explain musical ideas without using the vocabulary of music. So you can skip right to Chapter 2 and start playing. But remember when you come upon a term you don't know, you can always come back here and look it up.

How to Read Music

The concept of reading music has always been shrouded in mystery, but it doesn't have to be. Many guitarists have long reveled in the ease of tablature and eschewed the idea of reading standard notation, yet the basic skill of reading music can be summed up by two simple questions—"what notes do I play?" and "how long does each note last?"

The basics of reading are given here, while other hints are given at various points throughout the book. If you already know how to read music, you can skip the rest of this chapter and move on to Chapter 2.

The Music Alphabet

If reading music intimidates you, keep this in mind. While the alphabet has 26 letters, the music alphabet uses only seven different letter names: A B C D E F G. After G, the music alphabet starts over again at A. Only seven letters—how easy can it get!

How to Read Notes on a Staff

Music is written on a five-line grid called a *staff*. Notes are written on the lines, in addition to the spaces between the lines. There are five lines and four spaces, and they are counted from the bottom up. For example, the lowest line is referred to as the first line.

A *clef* indicates a reference note for the staff. Most guitar music uses the *treble* or *G clef*, which curls around the G note on the second line of the staff. This tells us that any note written on this line is G. From this note, we can find any other note by counting through the lines and spaces using the music alphabet. A *bar line* organizes the bar into rhythmic units called *measures* (or *bars*).

Treble Clef   Bar Line

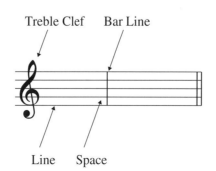

Line   Space

The notes on the staff are organized alphabetically corresponding to the music alphabet and in consecutive order of line-space-line, etc. A double bar line indicates the end of a piece or a section within a piece.

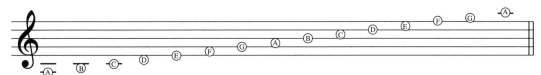

Notes on the staff are written from left to right, just like text. *Melodies* (notes played consecutively) are written horizontally and *harmonies* (notes played simultaneously) are written vertically.

Rhythmic Values of Notes

Here is a diagram of the most common note values.

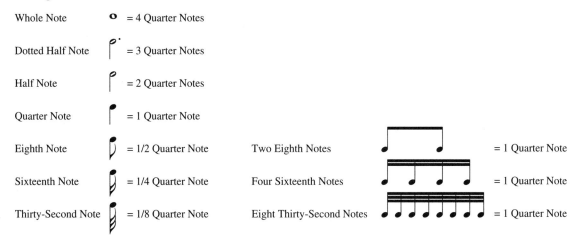

Adding a dot to any notehead or rest increases its duration by one-half of its original value (e.g., a dotted quarter note is equal in duration to one and one-half quarter notes, or three eighth notes).

Rests are measured silences. Whereas noteheads and stems indicate the amount of time a note is held, rests indicate the amount of time that silence is present. Here is a diagram of the most common rests.

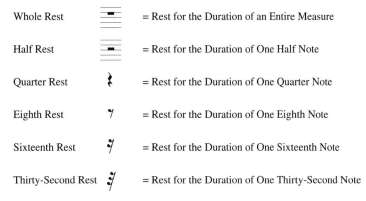

At the beginning of every piece of music is a *time signature*. The top number tells you how each bar of music is divided (e.g., 4 means there are four beats in each bar), and the bottom number tells which type of note equals one beat (4 means a quarter note, 8 means an eighth note, etc.).

9

In each time signature, different beats are *stressed* more (or played more strongly) than others. For instance, in 4/4 the first and third beats are accented, and in 3/4 only the first beat is accented. Stressed beats are called *downbeats,* while unstressed beats are called *upbeats.*

Ties are curved lines that connect consecutive notes of the same pitch and combine their durations. For instance, if two quarter notes are "tied," the result is equal to one half note. Only the first note of a tie is *attacked* (or played), while the others are simply sustained for the combined duration of the tied notes.

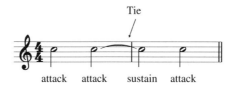

attack   attack   sustain   attack

Half Steps, Whole Steps, and Accidentals

The distance from one fret to the next is called a *half step.* A two-fret distance is called a *whole step.*

Notice the half steps and whole steps in the music alphabet. The only half steps that occur in the music alphabet are between B and C, and E and F. Here is a diagram containing the notes of the musical alphabet on the neck of a guitar.

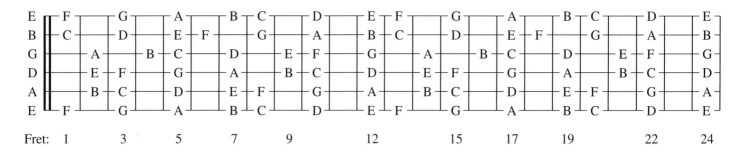

A *sharp* (♯) raises a note one half step (or one fret), while a *flat* (♭) lowers a note one half step (or one fret). For example, F is on the first fret of the high E string; F♯ is on the second fret. Sharps and flats apply for the duration of a bar. In other words, if you see a sharp before an F in a bar, any Fs on the same line of the staff that occur after it are sharp as well.

Any note that is sharp can also be re-named as a flat note and vice versa. This F♯ on the second fret of the high E string can also be called G♭. The note sounds the same, but it is named differently, depending upon its musical context.

Sharps and flats can be canceled by a *natural sign* (♮), which also applies for an entire bar.

The notes of the music alphabet, in combination with accidentals (sharps and flats), make up a total of twelve different notes.

1	2	3	4	5	6	7	8	9	10	11	12
A	A♯/B♭	B	C	C♯/D♭	D	D♯/E♭	E	F	F♯/G♭	G	G♯/A♭

Here is the guitar neck displayed with all the available notes:

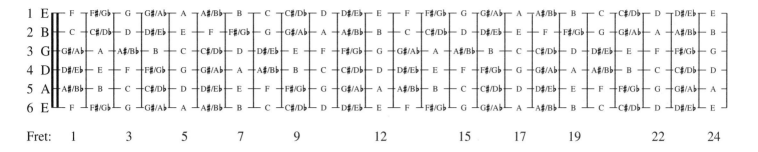

Key Signatures and Scales

Key signatures appear at the beginning of a line of music and indicate which notes must be sharped or flatted, as well as the key or *scale* of the piece. Sharp and flat symbols appear on the space or line of the notes that are to be affected, and they affect *all* notes that are of the same letter (e.g., all Bs, all Cs, etc.). For instance, you may find a piece of music that contains a key signature with a sharp symbol on the top line of the staff. This means that each F throughout the entire piece must be sharped.

A *scale* is a series of notes and is named according to the note on which it begins. For instance, a C scale begins on C, a G scale begins on G, etc. There are different types of scales, including *major*, *minor*, and *pentatonic* scales. You'll learn more about them in later chapters. For now, here is a table of common key signatures and the scales they can indicate:

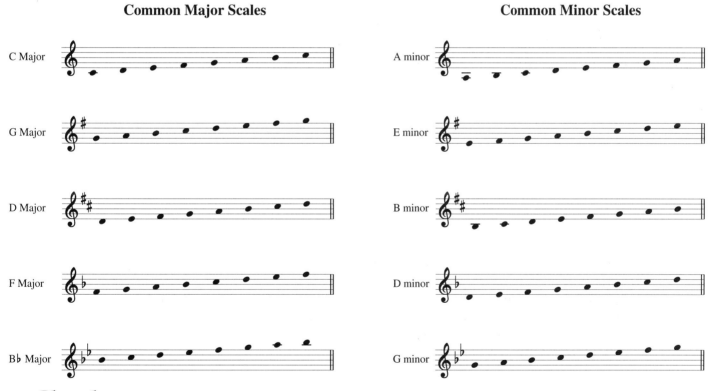

Chords

Chords are groups of notes that are based on scales. Most chords contain the first, third, and fifth members of a scale, plus perhaps other notes as well. For instance, a C major chord is built from those three degrees of the C major scale (C, E, and G), a G minor chord is made up of the first, third, and fifth degrees of a G minor scale (G, B♭, and D), and so forth. A *seventh chord* also contains a seventh degree of a scale.

Chord names generally appear above the music staff. A capital letter by itself indicates a major chord (e.g., "C"); if the letter is followed by an "m," it means it is a chord built on a minor scale (e.g., "Am"). A "7" indicates that it is a seventh chord (e.g., "G7," "Gm7," etc.).

CHAPTER 2

- **Power Chords**
- **Whole Notes**
- **Half Notes**
- **Quarter Notes**

Just making a chord sound good was the first cool thing [I did on the guitar]. —James Hetfield

One of the most important and easiest chord types to play is the *power chord*. With only two or three power chords, such as E5, A5, and D5, and a good sense of rhythm, you'll be rockin' away in no time—so "hit the lights" and let's get going!

A power chord is essentially a stripped-down version of a regular chord. Power chords are made up of only two or three low notes and provide a "heavy" sound.

Power chords come in two varieties: open position and moveable. An open position chord can be created using open strings and generally involves only the first few frets on the guitar, while a moveable chord contains no open strings.

The first power chord on our agenda is the open position E5 power chord, a 6th string-based power chord that is an absolute necessity for rock and perhaps one of the easiest chords you'll ever play. To play this chord, take the first finger of your left hand and press the second fret on the 5th string—this takes care of the left hand. Now, with your pick, downstroke the sixth and fifth strings together with your right hand and—*voila!* You have now taken the same first step as every rock guitarist who has gone before you.

E5

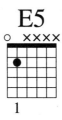

Note: It is normal to experience some pain in your left hand's fingertips. After some practice, you'll develop calluses which will provide resistance against the metal strings that are now digging deep crevices into your flesh! Also, when "fretting" the guitar neck, the best tone is produced by holding the string closer to the higher-numbered fret, rather than directly between the two frets. (See the photo at the beginning of Chapter 4 for an example of this.)

As you may recall from the previous chapter, a whole note is equal in duration to four quarter notes, and a half note is equal to two quarter notes. For now, think of the quarter note as equal to one beat in a measure.

So, now we're gonna have some fun with the E5 chord by playing some real Metallica riffs. We'll also work on reading and counting rhythms at the same time.

"Hit the Lights" Intro from *Kill 'Em All*

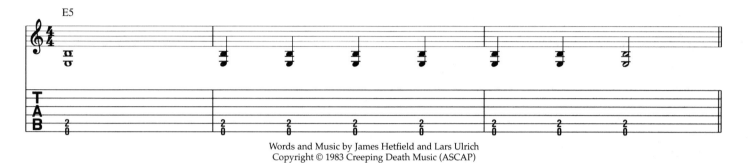

Words and Music by James Hetfield and Lars Ulrich
Copyright © 1983 Creeping Death Music (ASCAP)

The open position E5 chord is pretty easy. Well, good news—the open position A5 power chord is based on the same shape and is almost as easy—just start on the 5th string this time. Take your first finger and put it on the 2nd fret of the 4th string. Pick the 5th and 4th strings together—just be careful not to accidentally pick the 6th string!

A5

Switching between different chords is an essential skill required for almost every song. Let's practice switching between the A5 and E5 power chords. It's important not to get frustrated when attempting something like this for the first time. Everyone will probably feel as though their fingers are too unco-ordinated to shift chords quickly. Give it time, though, and before you know it, you won't even have to think about it.

"Phantom Lord" Post-Solo Interlude from *Kill 'Em All*

Words and Music by James Hetfield, Lars Ulrich and Dave Mustaine
Copyright © 1983 Creeping Death Music (ASCAP)

CHAPTER 3

- **Moveable Power Chords**
- **Ties**
- **Repeat Signs**
- **Eighth Notes**

Here are several power chords that begin on the 5th and 7th frets.

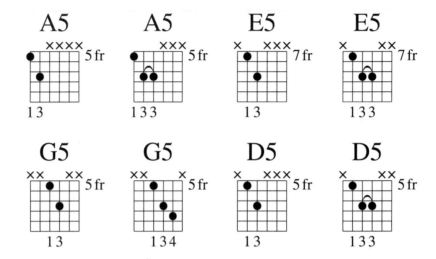

You may have noticed that a power chord is named according to the lowest note of the chord. For example, the open position E5 chord is named as such because the lowest note of the chord is the low E.

Let's try some examples that use moveable power chords. The example below also includes what is called a *tie*. In this "Master of Puppets" example, play that half note in measure 2, but let it ring for the duration of a half note plus a whole note (or six beats).

"Master of Puppets" Intro from *Master of Puppets*

Words and Music by James Hetfield, Lars Ulrich, Kirk Hammett and Cliff Burton
Copyright © 1986 Creeping Death Music (ASCAP)

The "Jump in the Fire" example below includes *repeat signs* (‖: :‖) which indicate that the bars between the signs are to be repeated—in other words, played again. It's that simple!

Eighth notes (♪♪♪♪ ♪♪♪♪) are counted in the following manner: say the beat number (1, 2, 3, or 4) for the *first* eighth of each beat, and the word "and" for the *second* eighth. For example:

1 and 2 and 3 and 4 and *etc.*

To help feel this rhythm, try verbalizing it using words that have two syllables, such as "pup-pet" or "sand-man." Compare and contrast this rhythm against a verbalized quarter note that has only one syllable, such as "one" or "lord."

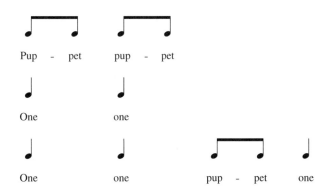

TRACK 5

"Jump in the Fire" Interlude from *Kill 'Em All*

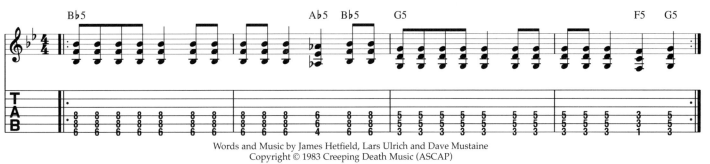

Words and Music by James Hetfield, Lars Ulrich and Dave Mustaine
Copyright © 1983 Creeping Death Music (ASCAP)

Now let's combine moveable power chords with the low E string. This texture of chords in combination with a low open string note is commonly used in rock and metal rhythm guitar. Note the *N.C.* in the example—it stands for "no chord" and indicates that no chords are to be strummed until the next chord is indicated.

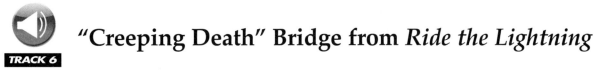

TRACK 6

"Creeping Death" Bridge from *Ride the Lightning*

Words and Music by James Hetfield, Lars Ulrich, Cliff Burton and Kirk Hammett
Copyright © 1984 Creeping Death Music (ASCAP)

CHAPTER 4

- ## Open Position Chords

There are two rhythm guitar parts in the next example. The first, a simplified part, uses power chords which you've already learned. The second rhythm guitar part uses *open position chords*, or chords that contain open-string notes.

When playing these open position chords, it is important to keep your left-hand fingers curved. This will ensure that none of your fretting fingers are muffling any open strings.

Left Hand Holding Open Position Chord

Before playing the second rhythm guitar part straight through, play each chord separately, making sure all the notes are ringing and clearly audible. Then practice switching between chords—first Am to C, then C to G, then G to Em, and finally from Em back to Am—concentrating on clarity and accuracy.

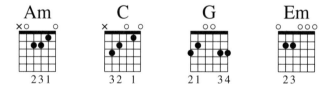

When you can comfortably switch between chords, try to play what is called a *rhythm part*. A rhythm part is a main background accompaniment as opposed to the solo guitar line. In the musical example on the following page, the rhythm part is played by both Guitar 1 and Guitar 2.

"Fade to Black" Verse from *Ride the Lightning*

Words and Music by James Hetfield, Lars Ulrich, Cliff Burton and Kirk Hammett
Copyright © 1984 Creeping Death Music (ASCAP)

You'll notice that, in many of these music examples, the vocals are included as a reference. Additional guitar parts are sometimes added as well. Unless otherwise noted, you should play the Guitar 1 part in each example. Once you've progressed through the book, you may want to go back and play the other parts as well.

CHAPTER 5

- **Eighth Notes Revisited**
- **Strumming Patterns**
- **Dotted Rhythms**
- **Anticipations**

Try this example which features a variety of eighth note/rest configurations.

"The Struggle Within" Intro from *Metallica*

Did you have a hard time coming in with that single eighth note in the first bar? If so, here's a trick: verbalize a bar of eight consecutive eighth notes, but leave out the syllable on the first eighth note of beat 2. Do it verbally as many times as you need to and really try to hear it in your head before playing the example again.

Here is an example with half, quarter, and eighth notes, plus ties.

TRACK 9

"Sad but True" Intro from *Metallica*

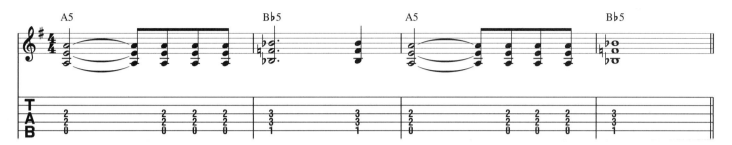

Strumming patterns are a way of notating the rhythm in which chords should be strummed. Chord symbols are shown with note value (duration) figures below to indicate the rhythm to be strummed by the right hand.

Here's how the intro from "Hit the Lights" would look written with strumming patterns. Compare this shorthand notation to the fully notated example on page 12.

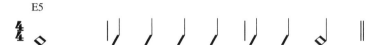

When playing full chords, it's best to use what is called *alternate strumming*. Use downstrokes (⊓) for the downbeats and upstrokes (v) for the upbeats. Alternate strumming can be notated like this: ⊓ v ⊓ v, ⊓ v ⊓ v.

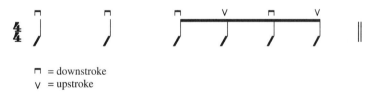

⊓ = downstroke
v = upstroke

For heavier, power chord-based music such as rock and metal, the best approach is to use down-strokes whenever possible. This helps provide a thicker and heavier sound.

Fast

Single eighth notes are also commonly paired with dotted quarter notes. A dotted quarter note lasts for a beat and a half (the equivalent of a quarter plus an eighth) or three eighths. This rhythm is tricky to play accurately, so verbalize it and listen carefully to the accompanying track.

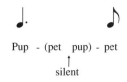

Pup - (pet   pup) - pet
↑
silent

"The Memory Remains" Intro from *Reload*

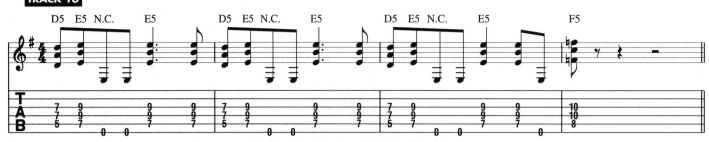

Words and Music by James Hetfield and Lars Ulrich
Copyright © 1997 Creeping Death Music (ASCAP)

"Fade to Black" Bridge from *Ride the Lightning*

Words and Music by James Hetfield, Lars Ulrich, Cliff Burton and Kirk Hammett
Copyright © 1984 Creeping Death Music (ASCAP)

In the second bar of the "Fade to Black" example, notice how the F♯ power chord falls on the upbeat of beat 3 rather than on beat 4. This is called an *anticipation* because it comes in earlier than expected, creating the illusion of a shifted downbeat. Anticipations add rhythmic variation and vitality to music.

Here are two more examples with anticipations.

"Creeping Death" Intro from *Ride the Lightning*

Words and Music by James Hetfield, Lars Ulrich, Cliff Burton and Kirk Hammett
Copyright © 1984 Creeping Death Music (ASCAP)

"Fight Fire with Fire" Interlude from *Ride the Lightning*

Words and Music by James Hetfield, Lars Ulrich and Cliff Burton
Copyright © 1984 Creeping Death Music (ASCAP)

CHAPTER 6

- ## Single Notes in Open Position

I think another first cool thing [I did on the guitar] was figuring out lines. It was just single note stuff. . . . You get a couple of notes right and get excited. And then do a couple of notes in a row.— James Hetfield

Now it's time to read music on the guitar. Before you get scared off and sell your guitar to the local pawnshop, keep in mind that it's not difficult at all. Even little kids can do it!

We will begin by examining the notes in open position. Each example has a rhythm guitar part, and some even have two rhythm guitar parts—an easy one and a more challenging one.

Here is a diagram of the natural notes (i.e., notes with no sharps or flats) in open position. Play through all the notes slowly, calling out their names as you go, starting on the low E and moving up to the G on the third fret of the 1st string.

The proper fingering for this exercise is as follows: the 1st finger plays notes indicated at the 1st fret, the 2nd finger plays notes indicated at the 2nd fret, the 3rd finger plays notes indicated at the 3rd fret, and the 4th finger plays notes indicated at the 4th fret. This diagram shows you how the notes on the staff fit on the guitar.

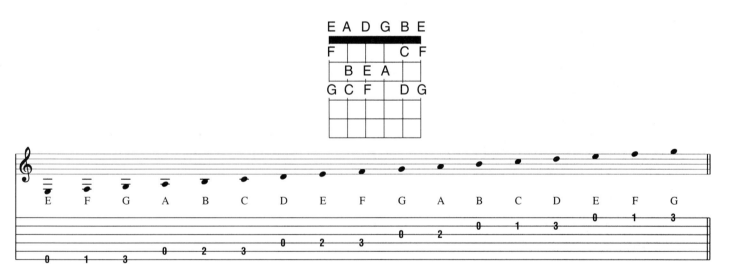

Let's work on reading some actual music now. In the next three examples, Guitar 1 contains the notes of only the high E string. Some are James' vocal lines, and some are his guitar riffs.

"One" Pre-Solo Interlude from . . . *And Justice for All*

TRACK 14

Words and Music by James Hetfield and Lars Ulrich
Copyright © 1988 Creeping Death Music (ASCAP)

"The Shortest Straw" Chorus from . . . *And Justice for All*

TRACK 15

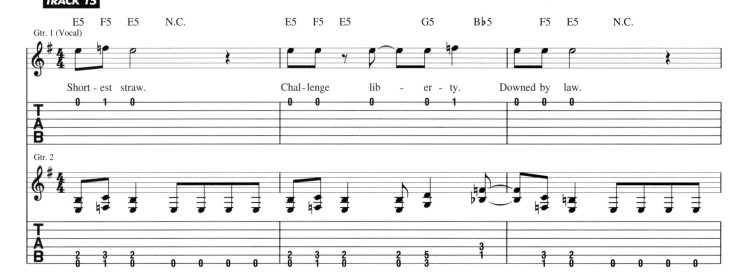

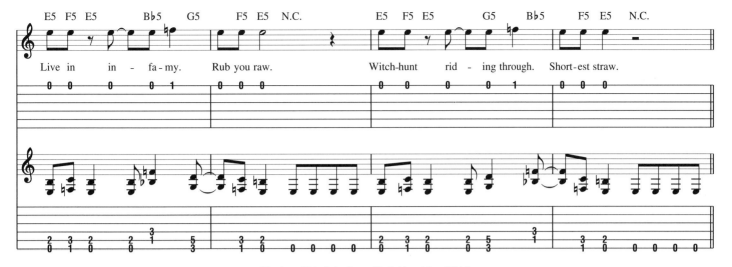

This example includes an F♯. Use your 2nd finger to fret this.

TRACK 16

"Damage, Inc." Verse from *Master of Puppets*

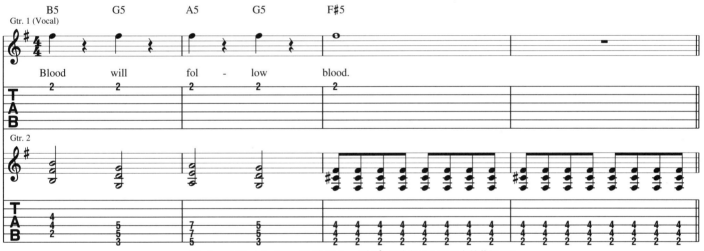

Now let's combine notes from the high E string with notes from the B string.

TRACK 17

"Wherever I May Roam" Intro from *Metallica*

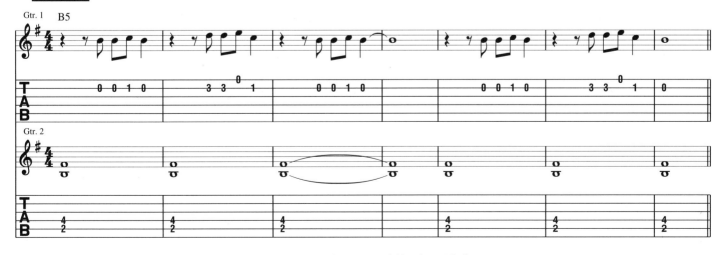

TRACK 18

"Battery" Intro from *Master of Puppets*

Words and Music by James Hetfield and Lars Ulrich
Copyright © 1986 Creeping Death Music (ASCAP)

These examples include notes from the G string.

TRACK 19

"Hero of the Day" Outro from *Load*

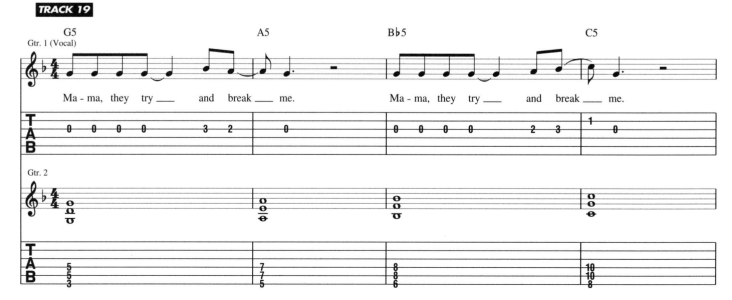

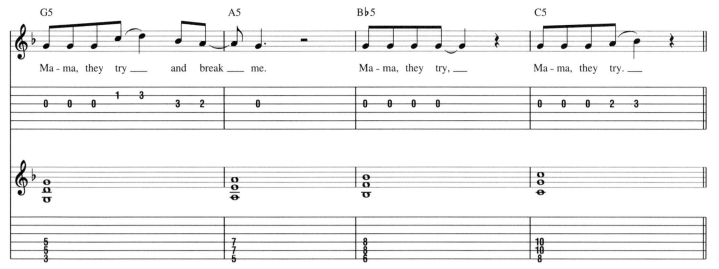

TRACK 20

"... And Justice for All" Chorus from ... *And Justice for All*

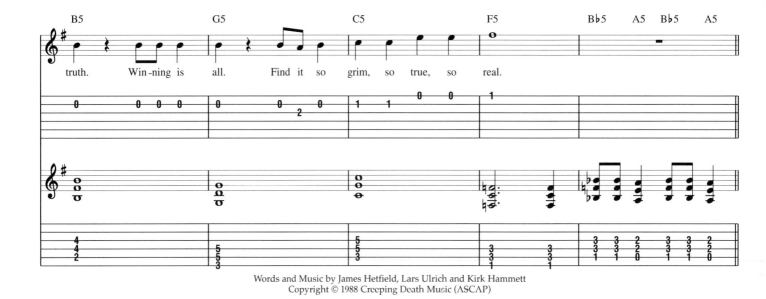

Now some notes from the D string.

"The Memory Remains" Bridge from *Reload*

Let's add the A string.

"The Four Horsemen" Pre-Solo Interlude Riff from *Kill 'Em All*

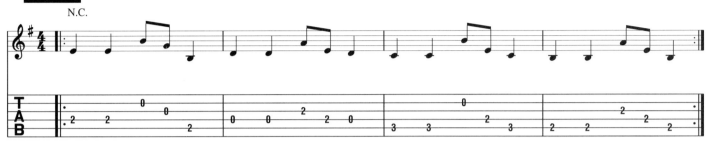

Words and Music by James Hetfield, Lars Ulrich and Dave Mustaine
Copyright © 1983 Creeping Death Music (ASCAP)

And now some notes from the low E string.

"Harvester of Sorrow" Intro from . . . *And Justice for All*

Words and Music by James Hetfield and Lars Ulrich
Copyright © 1988 Creeping Death Music (ASCAP)

CHAPTER 7

• **Sixteenth Notes**

One of the things that really identifies Metallica's music is its use of interesting rhythms. James Hetfield considers his guitar work to have a percussive role in the band:

I've always been pretty percussive on the guitar. I come up with a lot of parts for Lars to play as well. He's not writing all the drum parts, and sometimes he'll play something on the drums and I'll pick it up on the guitar. It's got to be percussive . . .—James Hetfield

Let's take a look at some more advanced rhythmic concepts that Metallica uses to distinguish itself as a rhythmically inventive band.

Sixteenth notes are four notes evenly spaced across a single quarter note (which also means that two sixteenth notes take up the same "space" as one eighth note). They are commonly verbalized as follows: say the beat number for the first sixteenth note of a group, followed by "e–and–a" for the three remaining sixteenth notes. For example:

1–e–and–a   2–e–and–a   3–e–and–a   4–e–and–a

You can also verbalize sixteenths into a four syllable word like "Un-for-giv-en." To accurately execute sixteenth notes, use strict alternate picking.

TRACK 24

"Eye of the Beholder" Verse Riff from . . . *And Justice for All*

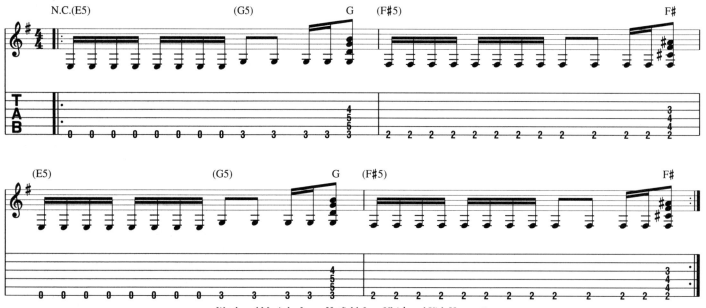

Words and Music by James Hetfield, Lars Ulrich and Kirk Hammett
Copyright © 1988 Creeping Death Music (ASCAP)

CHAPTER 8

- **Double Stops**
- **More on Chords**

In this chapter, we will look at some ways to combine notes on single strings. This first piece uses the notes of the E, B, G, and D strings in the Guitar 1 part.

E

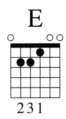

2 3 1

TRACK 25

"The Unforgiven" Intro from *Metallica*

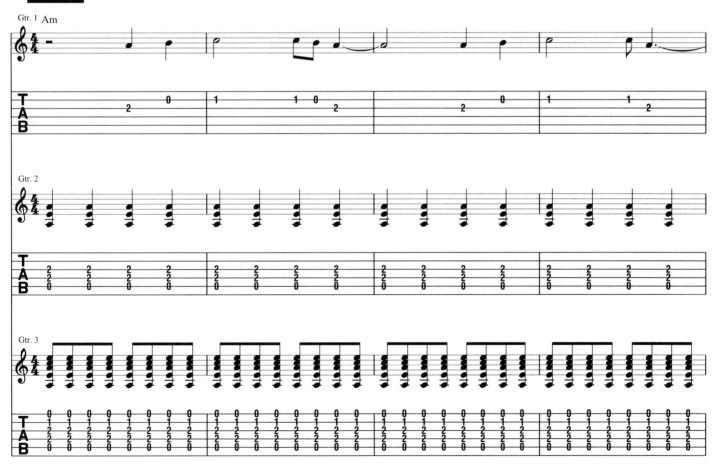

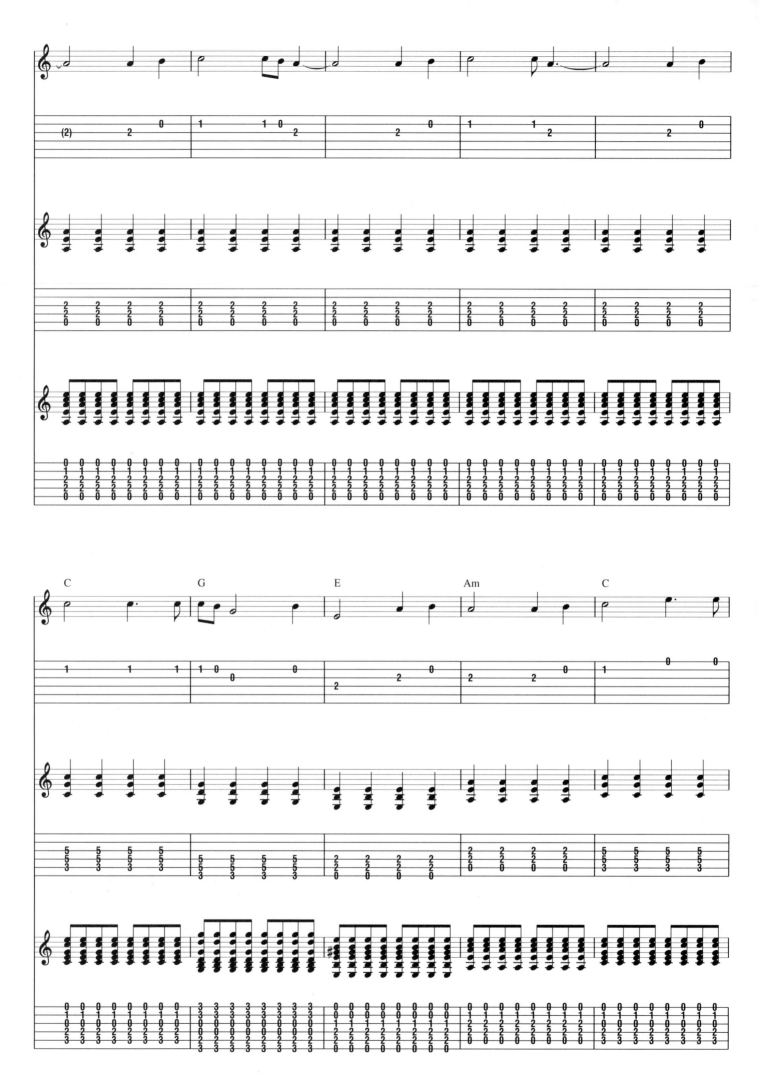

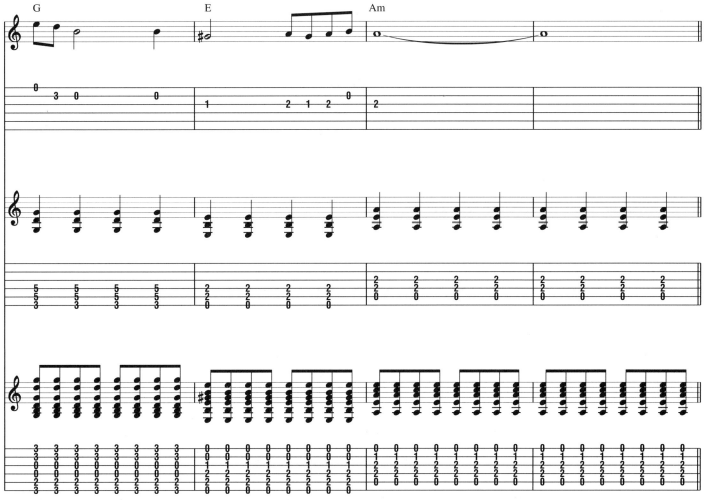

Words and Music by James Hetfield, Lars Ulrich and Kirk Hammett
Copyright © 1991 Creeping Death Music (ASCAP)

This next example makes use of *double stops*. Double stops are simply two notes played simultaneously. You may have noticed that you've already played some double stops—now you know what they are called!

TRACK 26

"Escape" Intro from *Ride the Lightning*

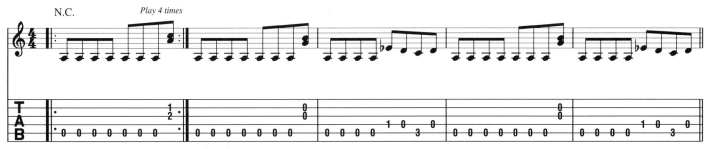

Words and Music by James Hetfield, Lars Ulrich and Kirk Hammett
Copyright © 1984 Creeping Death Music (ASCAP)

Here's a new chord, D minor, that you will often hear in Metallica's music. Try playing the Guitar 2 part.

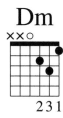

Dm

TRACK 27

"Mama Said" Verse from *Load*

Words and Music by James Hetfield and Lars Ulrich
Copyright © 1996 Creeping Death Music (ASCAP)

32

Now that you've played notes on all of the strings in open position, here's an extended example so you can practice your new skills. The second rhythm guitar part in the verse is based on an Am chord shape and has lots of *syncopation,* or accented upbeats. The best way to play this part is to form the Am chord with your left hand and finger the non-chord notes around this shape. The D and B notes on the 2nd string and the open G string can all be easily played by adding or lifting a left-hand finger from the chord.

In the chorus, be careful with the double stops. The first bar has double stops based on the Am chord shape and is most efficiently played by holding onto the Am shape. The second bar contains a double stop figure that is best approached by holding the shape of the double stop on the 3rd and 4th strings with the 1st and 2nd left-hand fingers, and then adding and removing the 3rd finger to catch and release the next double stop note on the 3rd string. These two bars make up the bulk of the rhythm guitar part for the chorus. Try playing all three parts slowly, one after the other, until you can play them up to speed.

TRACK 28

"Until It Sleeps" Intro from *Load*

And the pain ___ still hates ___ me, ___ so hold ___ me un - til ___ it sleeps. ___

Words and Music by James Hetfield and Lars Ulrich
Copyright © 1996 Creeping Death Music (ASCAP)

CHAPTER 9

- **Barre Chords**
- **Slides**
- **Triplets**

Barre chords are those in which you use one finger to cover two or more strings across the same fret. The most common barre chords are based on the open position chords E, Em, E7, A, Am, and A7. The shape of a barre chord resembles that of its open position cousin with a barre holding down what were originally the open strings.

Here are some useful barre chords for you to learn. They are shown with their non-barred equivalents.

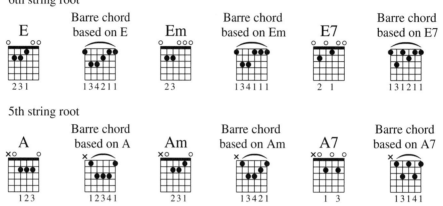

To play a barre chord, flatten your first finger across the strings for which the barre is indicated. The common problem for people just learning barre chords is that some of the strings do not ring clearly. This is because either the first finger is not holding them down strongly enough or because other fingers are in the way. You should isolate which string is not ringing and adjust your technique accordingly, pressing harder with the first finger or arching the fingers more to get them out of the way. Barre chords require considerable strength in the fingers, which is most likely underdeveloped in a beginning player. With lots of practice, it will all start to feel natural after a while.

Before playing the next example in tempo, isolate the chords and work on connecting them individually, as when you were learning open chords.

An "x" tells you to mute a string by holding it lightly with your left hand so as stop it from ringing and produce a chunky, percussive sound. Those diagonal lines indicate slides. With a slide, you literally slide a fretting finger up or down on a string from one note to another. When you see a slide that has a starting note but no destination, slide your finger up or down just a few frets from the note, gradually releasing pressure, and then take it off the fretboard as usual in order to finger the next note. As you can see in the following example, you can slide more than one note at a time.

"To Live Is to Die" Intro Riff from ... *And Justice for All*

TRACK 29

Triplets are groups of three notes normally played in the space of two and are commonly verbalized by saying the beat number for the first triplet note, followed by "and–a" for the two remaining notes. For example:

1–and–a 2–and–a 3–and–a 4–and–a

Triplets can also be verbalized into a three syllable word like "Bat-ter-y!" To play them, you can use either strict alternate picking or triplet picking (⊓ V ⊓, ⊓ V ⊓). Triplets can be very difficult to master when you are first learning to read and play. Up until now, you've been used to counting even numbers of notes per beat. First, notice how they're notated. Then, listen carefully to the example in order to get a feel for triplets. Finally, try to play them yourself.

"One" Pre-Solo Interlude from . . . *And Justice for All*

Words and Music by James Hetfield and Lars Ulrich
Copyright © 1988 Creeping Death Music (ASCAP)

CHAPTER 10

• Major and Minor Scales

Scales are series of notes used as resources for creating melodies and harmonies. The major and minor scales are two important scales to learn.

One good example of a major scale is the C major scale. It contains no accidentals (sharps or flats) and is made up of the notes C, D, E, F, G, A, B (starting over on the next C). Notice that there are whole steps (or two frets) between all notes except E and F (the 3rd and 4th degrees of the scale), as well as B and C (the 7th and 8th degrees), which are separated by one half step (or one fret) each. This arrangement of half and whole steps is what makes a scale major.

An easy minor scale to learn is the A minor scale. It also contains no accidentals and is made up of the notes A, B, C, D, E, F, G (starting over again on the next A). Here, there are whole steps between all notes except B and C (the 2nd and 3rd degrees of the scale), as well as E and F (the 5th and 6th degrees).

Here are three of the most common moveable patterns for several scales. Practice these patterns slowly, going up and down the scales until the fingerings are ingrained into your muscle memory.

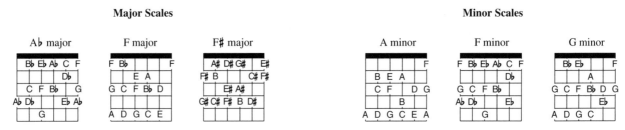

Here are some major scale ideas. This first one includes portions of the A major scale and is a very common and easily recognizable pattern. It also makes a great finger exercise or a flashy, show-stopping lick.

TRACK 31

"The Call of Ktulu" Solo from *Ride the Lightning*

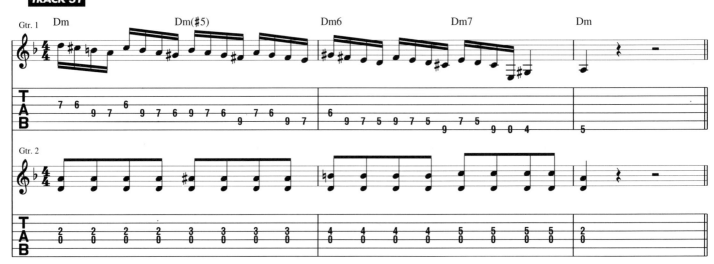

Words and Music by James Hetfield, Lars Ulrich, Cliff Burton and Dave Mustaine
Copyright © 1984 Creeping Death Music (ASCAP)

This example includes portions of the G major scale in the context of a solo. It shows how scales are used melodically.

TRACK 32

"Fade to Black" Solo from *Ride the Lightning*

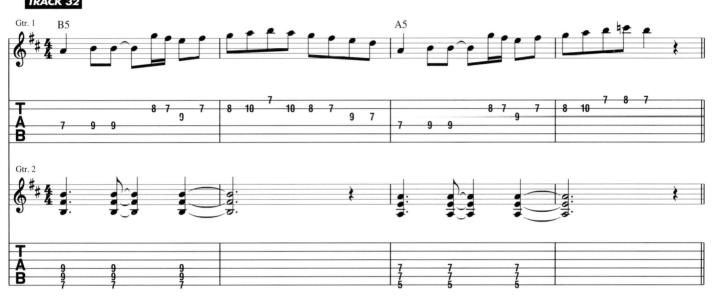

Words and Music by James Hetfield, Lars Ulrich, Cliff Burton and Kirk Hammett
Copyright © 1984 Creeping Death Music (ASCAP)

Here are some minor scale ideas.

This example includes an A minor scale played almost entirely with alternating downstrokes and upstrokes.

TRACK 33

"Fade to Black" Intro from *Ride the Lightning*

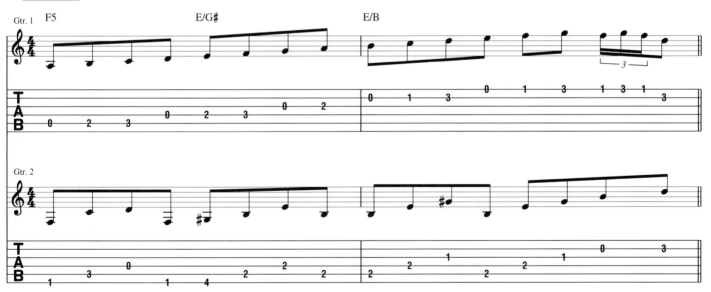

Words and Music by James Hetfield, Lars Ulrich, Cliff Burton and Kirk Hammett
Copyright © 1984 Creeping Death Music (ASCAP)

This example includes portions of the B minor scale.

TRACK 34

"Frayed Ends of Sanity" Interlude from . . . *And Justice for All*

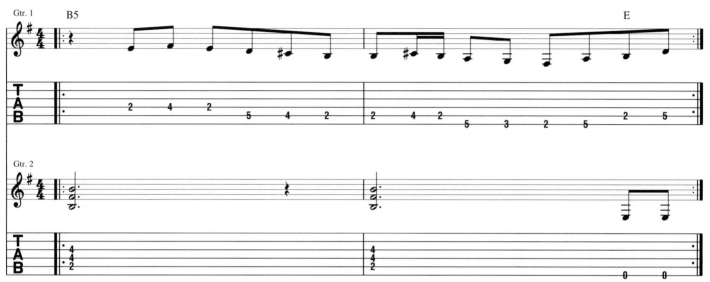

Words and Music by James Hetfield, Lars Ulrich and Kirk Hammett
Copyright © 1988 Creeping Death Music (ASCAP)

With this example, you'll have to slide two frets out of position to catch the next-to-last D note on the 10th fret of the high E string.

TRACK 35

"Fight Fire with Fire" Intro from *Ride the Lightning*

Words and Music by James Hetfield, Lars Ulrich and Cliff Burton
Copyright © 1984 Creeping Death Music (ASCAP)

CHAPTER 11

- ## Pentatonic Minor Scales
- ## Blues Scales

The scales of choice for rock and roll, past and present, are unquestionably the pentatonic minor and blues scales. These scales are the bases for countless riffs, licks, and runs, and are used by virtually every guitarist.

> *If I got a lick, that was 100% gratification. If I got the feel, that was just as good. Or if I got inspired off it, that was good, too.* —Kirk Hammet

Whereas the major and natural minor scales are more often used for generating lyrical, singable melodies and serve as foundations for creating harmonies, the pentatonic minor and blues scales are used primarily to create riffs and licks.

Here are examples of scales and patterns for the pentatonic minor and blues scales starting on E and based on open position fingering.

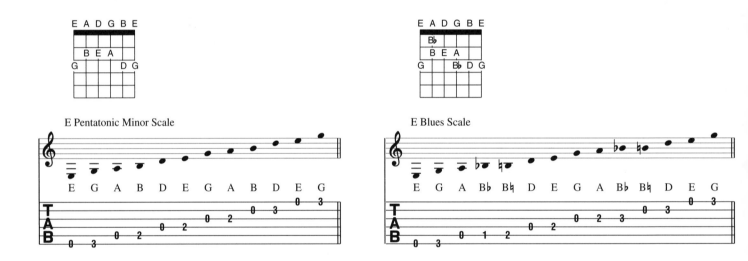

Let's try some riffs based on these scales. After playing through some of these examples, try creating your own riffs using these scales.

Here's an E pentatonic minor example.

TRACK 36

"Bad Seed" Intro Riff from *Reload*

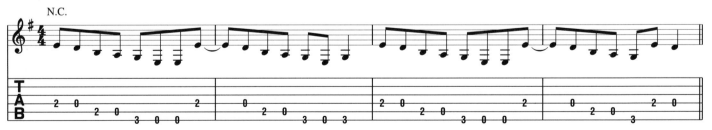

Words and Music by James Hetfield, Lars Ulrich and Kirk Hammett
Copyright © 1997 Creeping Death Music (ASCAP)

And now an E blues example.

"Enter Sandman" Intro Riff from *Metallica*

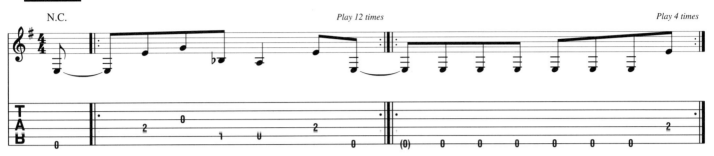

Double stops can also be created from these scales. Here's an example using the E blues scale.

"Seek and Destroy" Intro Riff #2 from *Kill 'Em All*

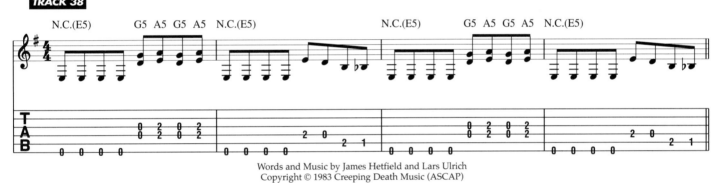

Sometimes power chords are combined with these scales. Here's another example with the E blues scale.

"Sad but True" Intro Riff from *Metallica*

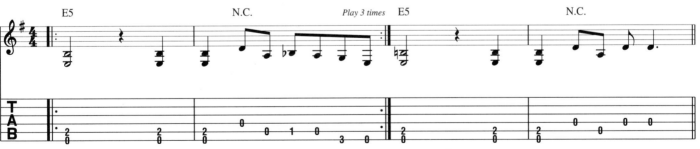

CHAPTER 12

• Bending, Vibrato, Slides

I just hit a point on the last tour where I was bored with my playing, and it bummed me out. But playing different stuff every night keeps it exciting. To tap into that reservoir, I practice different things. Wanna play fast? You have to have the speed. If you want to play subdued, real slow vibrato, you have to have that vibrato.—Kirk Hammett

Now that your guitar can talk, let's make it sing and scream. The articulation of notes on the guitar determines how the music comes across to the listener. Imagine two different people reciting the Declaration of Independence, with the first person speaking in a nervous, *staccato* (meaning that each sound is very short and defined, or "clipped"), rapid-fire, manner and the second person speaking in a monotone, flowing, almost comatose drawl. While the passage is the same, the two people sound totally different because of their articulations. And it is their articulations that give them their identities. It's the same case in music.

On the guitar, there are several expressive techniques that allow you to put your own unique stamp on anything you play. That's what it means to play "with feeling" or to have a "nice touch." Believe it or not, you've already learned one articulation technique—the slide. Here are a few others.

Bending a note is pushing or pulling a string with the fretting hand to raise the pitch. When you bend a note, it is important that it is bent with a destination note in mind. Your bend may sound out of tune if you go too far or not far enough. In music notation, the distance of a bend is measured in reference to a whole step (a two-fret distance). For example, the fraction "1/2" next to a bend indicates a half step bend, while the number "1" indicates a whole step bend.

Here is an E pentatonic minor riff that uses bending.

"No Remorse" Pre-Chorus from *Kill 'Em All*

Words and Music by James Hetfield and Lars Ulrich
Copyright © 1983 Creeping Death Music (ASCAP)

Vibrato is an expressive technique that is similar to bending. Vibrato is created by the rapid, continual bending and releasing of a note. This constant back-and-forth movement allows long notes to sustain and gives life to shorter notes. A vibrato is indicated with a wavy line.

"Bleeding Me" Intro Riff from *Load*

Words and Music by James Hetfield, Lars Ulrich and Kirk Hammett
Copyright © 1996 Creeping Death Music (ASCAP)

If you're having problems creating vibrato, make sure to anchor your left hand on the neck of the guitar. This will give you more control as you bend the string.

CHAPTER 13

- **Hammer-Ons**
- **Pull-Offs**

Hammer-ons and pull-offs can be used to play two consecutive notes on the same string with a single pick stroke; they can make good alternatives to picking every single note. A hammer-on is executed by picking the first note and then using another left-hand finger to strike "hammer" the second note higher on the string. Only the first note (the lower note) is picked.

A pull-off is executed by using a finger that is fretting a note to pluck the string as it leaves the fretboard. This plucking of the string causes a lower note to sound, eliminating the need for right-hand picking. Only the first note (the higher note) is picked.

With an open-string pull-off (as in the examples), finger the first note with the left hand, pluck it with the pick, and then pull your finger off the neck so that the open-string note sounds. With other pull-offs, place one left-hand finger on the fret of the first (higher) note and another on the second (lower) note; pluck the first note with the pick and then pluck with the left-hand finger while removing it from the string, causing the second note to sound.

These examples use hammer-ons and pull-offs. The notation for both looks like a tie. If the curved line connects a first note to a second note with a higher pitch, it is indicating a hammer-on. If the second note is lower in pitch than the first, it is a pull-off. If the notes are of the same pitch, it is a tie.

TRACK 42

"Fuel" Intro Riff from *Reload*

TRACK 43

"Fuel" Intro Riff from *Reload*

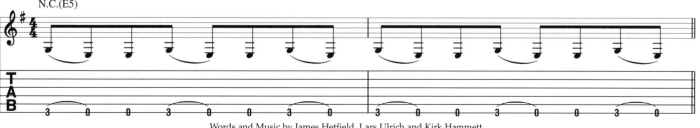

If you're having problems getting your hammer-ons and pull-offs to sound correctly (strings are buzzing or sounding muted), make doubly sure that the fingers of your left hand are fretting the notes very firmly. With a pull-off, make sure that the finger you remove from the fretboard is plucking the string sufficiently.

CHAPTER 14

- **Moveable Pentatonic Minor Scales**
- **Moveable Blues Scales**

Pentatonic minor and blues scales are moveable. Let's take the open position E pentatonic minor and blues scales and move them to a different key—say, G. Since the root is always on the 6th string, all we have to do is move the shapes up to the G on the 3rd fret of the 6th string. As the open position E pentatonic minor and blues scales made use of open strings, we will have to use the 1st finger to replace whatever was open.

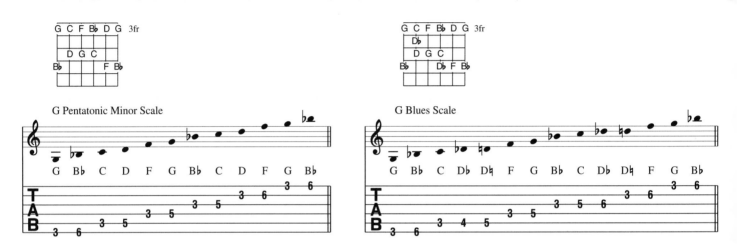

The finger patterns of the pentatonic minor and blues scales are often referred to as *boxes* because of their shapes. Take a look at your left-hand fingers as you play these scales and you'll see this. This visual association makes memorization relatively easy, and after learning a few riffs and licks, using these scales will become automatic.

Here is a G blues scale riff.

"Jump in the Fire" Intro Riff from *Kill 'Em All*

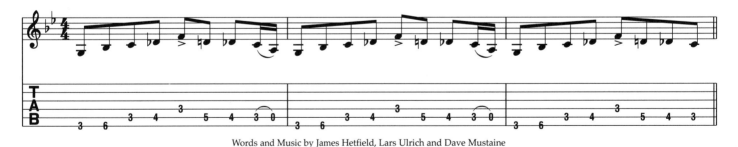

Words and Music by James Hetfield, Lars Ulrich and Dave Mustaine
Copyright © 1983 Creeping Death Music (ASCAP)

And a G pentatonic minor lick.

"Jump in the Fire" Lick from *Kill 'Em All*

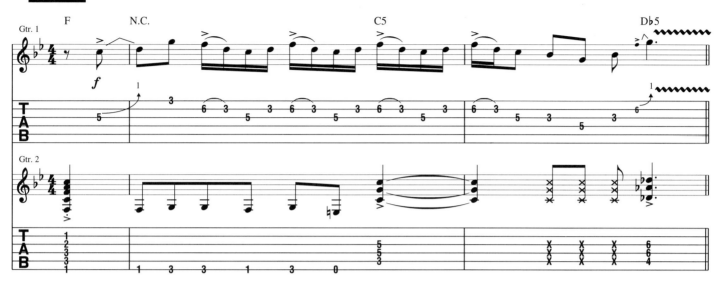

Here are some classic pentatonic minor and blues lead licks that are used by virtually every lead guitarist. Learn these licks and try to integrate them into your own playing. At first, it may sound awkward or contrived just to plop licks down in a "connect-the-dots" manner, but eventually they will become part of your musical vocabulary and will flow naturally and spontaneously.

These licks are based on the B pentatonic minor and blues scales, also known as *7th fret boxes* because the left-hand fingering begins at the 7th fret.

"Fade to Black" Solo from *Ride the Lightning*

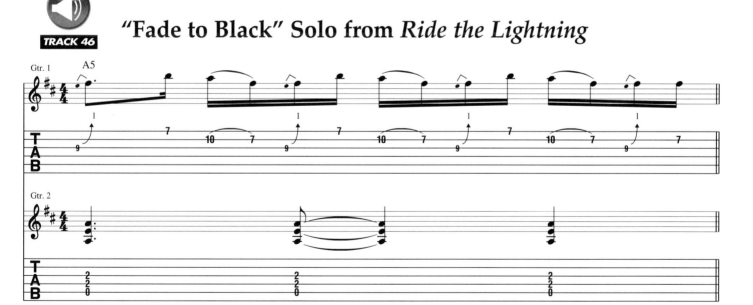

"Hit the Lights" Solo from *Kill 'Em All*

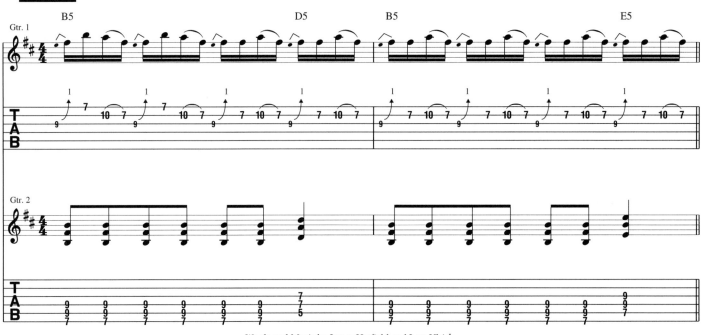

TRACK 48

"Fade to Black" Solo from *Ride the Lightning*

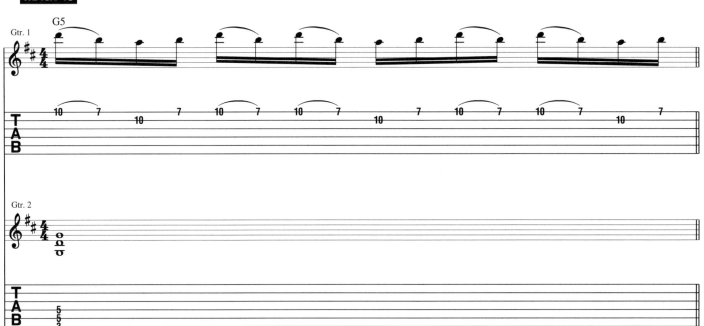

TRACK 49

"Orion" Solo from *Master of Puppets*

Words and Music by James Hetfield, Lars Ulrich and Cliff Burton
Copyright © 1986 Creeping Death Music (ASCAP)

TRACK 50

"Orion" Solo from *Master of Puppets*

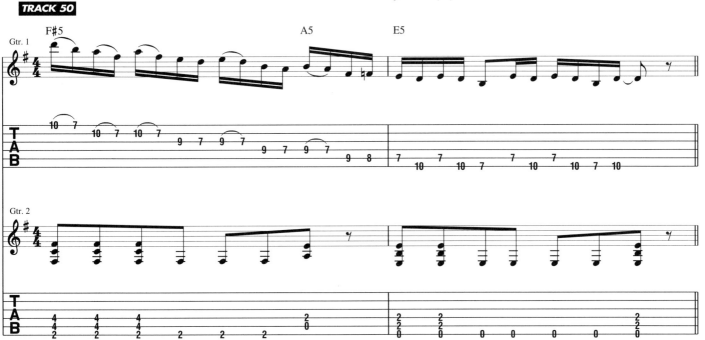

Words and Music by James Hetfield, Lars Ulrich and Cliff Burton
Copyright © 1986 Creeping Death Music (ASCAP)

CHAPTER 15

• **Second Position**

Reading in 2nd position is similar to reading in open position. The only differences are that, in 2nd position, there are no open strings, fingerings begin on the 2nd fret, and a new note is introduced—the A on the 5th fret of the high E string.

When you are playing in 2nd position, your first finger plays all notes on the 2nd fret, your 2nd finger plays all notes on the 3rd fret, your 3rd finger plays all notes on the 4th fret, and your 4th finger plays all notes on the 5th fret. This diagram shows the notes in 2nd position.

Notes in 2nd Position

Here is a reading example from an earlier chapter. The notes are the same, but now Guitar 1 should be played in 2nd position.

TRACK 51

"Battery" Intro Riff from *Master of Puppets*

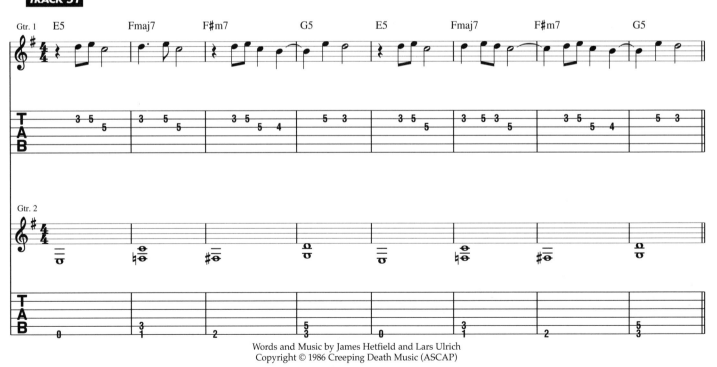

Words and Music by James Hetfield and Lars Ulrich
Copyright © 1986 Creeping Death Music (ASCAP)

Since open strings tend to have a more "ringing" sound than fretted ones, playing single-note passages exclusively with fretted notes will provide a more uniform *timbre* (tone quality).

Here are two examples where Guitar 1 is played in 2nd position.

TRACK 52

"Leper Messiah" Interlude from *Master of Puppets*

"To Live Is to Die" Intro Riff from . . . *And Justice for All*

Words and Music by James Hetfield, Lars Ulrich and Cliff Burton
Copyright © 1988 Creeping Death Music (ASCAP)

This example combines notes from 2nd position with the open G and A strings. The indication *let ring* means that you should let the notes ring out without stopping or dampening them, while *sim.* (which stands for "simile") means, essentially, "continue in the same manner as previously." A *sim.* marking is often used instead of repeating directions over and over again within a piece of music. In this instance, it indicates that the *let ring* indication applies to each measure in this example.

TRACK 54

"Fade to Black" Intro from *Ride the Lightning*

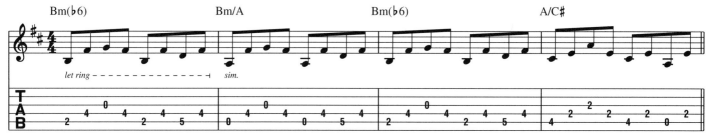

Words and Music by James Hetfield, Lars Ulrich, Cliff Burton and Kirk Hammett
Copyright © 1984 Creeping Death Music (ASCAP)

CHAPTER 16

- **Fifth Position**
- **Palm Muting**

Here are the notes in 5th position. The range is extended up to the C on the 8th fret of the high E string.

Notes in 5th Position

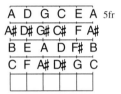

Let's see what our earlier open position and 2nd position example looks like in 5th position.

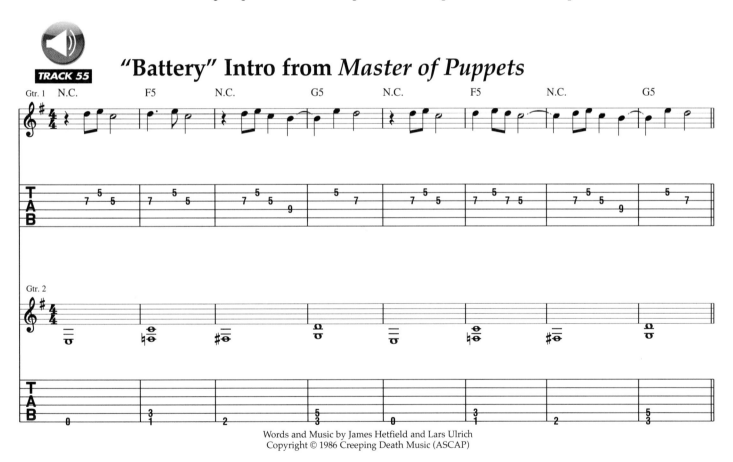

"Battery" Intro from *Master of Puppets*

Words and Music by James Hetfield and Lars Ulrich
Copyright © 1986 Creeping Death Music (ASCAP)

Let's do some more reading in 5th position.

This first example has a repeat sign with a numbered ending bracket, indicating that there is more than one ending for the excerpt. The first time through, play the example up to the repeat sign under the first ending bracket ("1."), then repeat the entire selection until you come to the bracketed section again. This time, skip over any music under the first ending bracket and head directly to the music under the second ending bracket ("2."). Using numbered ending brackets eliminates the need to copy entire sections of repeated music just to accommodate an ending that is different.

Both the Guitar 1 and 2 parts here are to be played in 5th position.

TRACK 56 **"Fight Fire with Fire" Interlude from *Ride the Lightning***

Words and Music by James Hetfield, Lars Ulrich and Cliff Burton
Copyright © 1984 Creeping Death Music (ASCAP)

In this next example, the first three endings are the same (indicated by the numbers under the bracket), followed by a conclusive fourth ending. Again, both the Guitar 1 and 2 parts here are to be played in 5th position.

TRACK 57

"Ride the Lightning" Intro from *Ride the Lightning*

Here are two more examples with which you can practice reading. As before, the Guitar 1 and 2 parts are to be played in 5th position.

TRACK 58

"The Struggle Within" Intro from *Metallica*

"Sad but True" Interlude from *Metallica*

Words and Music by James Hetfield and Lars Ulrich
Copyright © 1991 Creeping Death Music (ASCAP)

This next example uses a technique called *palm muting*, indicated by a "P.M." between the notation and tablature staves. Palm muting anchors the right hand against the bridge, so that any note that gets picked is slightly muffled by the right-hand palm. Dotted lines show the duration of the palm mute.

Also, notice the accent marks (>) in this excerpt. An accent mark tells you where to put an emphasis or stress (i.e., play the note a little louder and harder). You may also notice that this piece makes use of some of the pentatonic minor and blues scale licks that we've covered.

"Jump in the Fire" Solo from *Kill 'Em All*

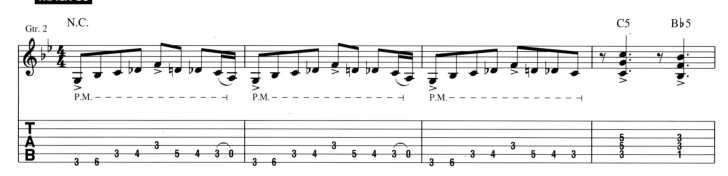

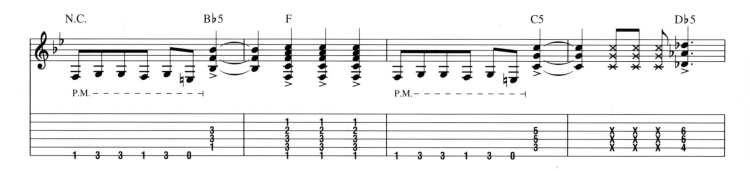

So come on! __

Jump in the fire! __

Words and Music by James Hetfield, Lars Ulrich and Dave Mustaine
Copyright © 1983 Creeping Death Music (ASCAP)

C HAPTER 17

- **Fingerpicking**

Fingerpicking is a technique used in folk and classical music. When you fingerpick, you pluck the strings with your fingers instead of striking them with a pick. Using the right hand in this way enables you to play two lines simultaneously or to pluck all of the notes of a chord at once.

Four of the fingers of your right hand are used for fingerpicking, and each have a corresponding letter that indicates each within a piece of music. These are: thumb (p), index (i), middle (m), and ring (a). The pinky is normally not used. Conventionally, the thumb plucks downward (towards the floor) on a lower string to sound a bass note, while the other fingers pluck upwards (towards the ceiling) on the upper strings.

This example is in 6/8, meaning each bar contains the rhythmic equivalent of six eighth notes.

"Nothing Else Matters" Intro from *Metallica*

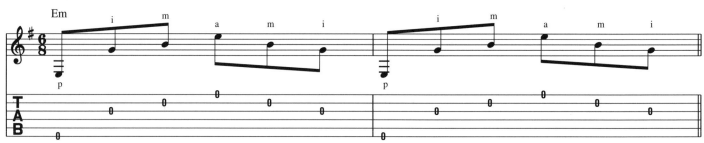

Words and Music by James Hetfield and Lars Ulrich
Copyright © 1991 Creeping Death Music (ASCAP)

To play the two examples on the next page, hold down the shape of a chord with the left hand and slowly practice the fingerpicking pattern with the fingers of your right hand, making sure you are using the correct finger indicated for each note. After this feels comfortable, practice changing chords while keeping the right-hand pattern in motion.

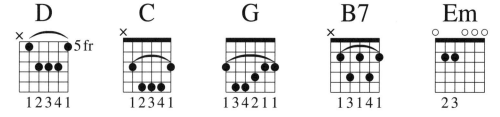

"Nothing Else Matters" Intro from *Metallica*

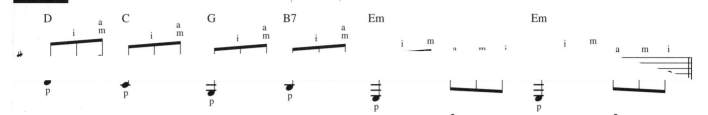

Words and Music by James Hetfield and Lars Ulrich
Copyright © 1991 Creeping Death Music (ASCAP)

Here's a final example for you. By this point, you should really feel like you've accomplished something. Think about where you were when you began this book! Hold down these chord shapes as you play the example:

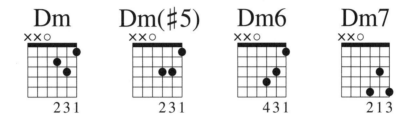

"The Call of Ktulu" Intro Riff from *Ride the Lightning*

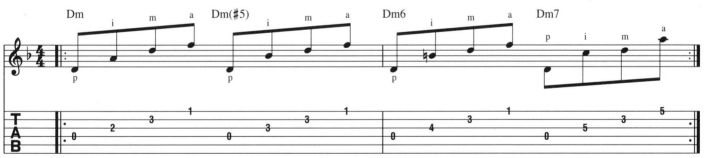

Words and Music by James Hetfield, Lars Ulrich, Cliff Burton and Dave Mustaine
Copyright © 1984 Creeping Death Music (ASCAP)

Well, there's times when I'm feeling like something is missing. I start questioning what I'm doing in my life, and then all of a sudden I'll remember that I haven't picked up my guitar for a couple of weeks or a month. I go, "Oh yeah, I've been on vacation from the band. That doesn't mean I shouldn't play guitar. That's part of me," and I pick up the guitar and instantly create a little something and feel 100% better. —James Hetfield

Now that you've mastered the music in *Learn to Play Guitar with Metallica*, you're ready to take on more difficult pieces. You may want to try playing other guitar solos from Metallica's music or that of other heavy metal groups, or you may wish to work through more advanced instructional books or collections of licks and riffs. You may even decide to take lessons. Whatever you do, you'll find that the techniques you've learned in this book will serve you well. Good luck!